Rang

GW00373984

TRÁLÍ.

I remember,
I remember

Brian Moses lives on the Sussex coast with his wife
and two daughters. He writes and edits poetry for
young people. He travels extensively both in the UK
and abroad, presenting his poetry and percussion
shows in schools and libraries. Two books of his own
poetry – *Barking Back at Dogs* and *Don't Look at Me
in That Tone of Voice!* – are also published by
Macmillan.

Other books by Macmillan

BARKING BACK AT DOGS
Poems by Brian Moses

DON'T LOOK AT ME IN THAT TONE OF VOICE!
Poems by Brian Moses

SCOTTISH POEMS
Poems chosen by John Rice

OVERHEARD ON A SALTMARSH
Poems chosen by Carol Ann Duffy

LOVE
Poems chosen by Fiona Waters

SARDINES
Poems by Stephen Knight

I remember,
I remember

a celebration of childhood in verse

Edited by Brian Moses

MACMILLAN CHILDREN'S BOOKS

First published 2003 by Macmillan Children's Books
a division of Macmillan Publishers Limited
20 New Wharf Road, London N1 9RR
Basingstoke and Oxford
www.panmacmillan.com

Associated companies throughout the world

ISBN 0 330 43393 8

1 3 5 7 9 8 6 4 2

A CIP catalogue record for this book is available from the British Library.

Printed and bound in Great Britain by Mackays of Chatham plc, Kent

For my mother, and in memory of my father –
for the magic of my childhood

'There must be a place under the sun,
where hearts of olden glory grow young'

Runrig

Contents

I Remember, I Remember   *Thomas Hood*   2

A Place Without Footprints

Do We Know?	*David Greygoose*	6
Going Down	*Helen Lamb*	7
The Special Place	*Jennifer Curry*	8
If Once You have Slept on an Island	*Rachel Field*	10
The Shining	*Brian Lee*	12
Boy on the Beach	*Eric Finney*	14
Midsummer Magic	*Patricia Leighton*	15
In the Moonlight	*Eric Finney*	18
Home	*Philip Waddell*	20
Until We Built a Cabin	*Aileen Fisher*	21
The Shooting Stars	*James Carter*	22
A Place Without Footprints	*Daphne Kitching*	24

The Music of Dripping Stones

The Well	*Kenneth C. Steven*	28
Mapping Our World	*Linda Newbery*	30
The Tunnel	*Brian Lee*	32
Summer in Brooklyn	*Lawrence Ferlinghetti*	34

The Old Canal   Geoffrey Summerfield   36
Heatwave Summer   Cathy Warry   41
Being Late   Mary Green   42
Going   Brian Lee   44
By St Thomas Water   Charles Causley   47
Ice   Jim Wong-Chu   51

Such a World Comes In

Doing Nothing Much   Eric Finney   54
Dad's Shed   Matt Simpson   55
Den to Let   Gareth Owen   57
Once Upon a Time and Space   Mike Johnson   61
The Christmas Shed   Wes Magee   63
Singing in the Streets   James Reeves   65
Snow Spell   Berlie Doherty   67
Requiem for a Robin   Sue Cowling   68
from Growing Up Alone   Robert Adamson   69
The Magic of the Brain   Jenny Joseph   70

The White Ball Never Fell . . .

My Old Jumper   John Coldwell   74
Street Cricket   Gareth Owen   75
A Better Game   John Mole   77
Hill Rolling   Andrew Taylor   79
Conker Crazy   Pie Corbett   80
Fishing Summer   Brian Moses   82

The Ascent of Everest	*David Whitehead*	84
Little Houses	*Angela Topping*	87
The Magical Bicycle	*Berlie Doherty*	88
Paradise	*John Mole*	92
Hiding Places	*Sue Dymoke*	93
Well Hidden	*Dave Calder*	95
Game's End	*David Sutton*	97
The Blue Marble	*Tony Mitton*	98

If There is a Train to Paradise

About Friends	*Brian Jones*	100
Cranky, Scotty, Mooey and Me	*Steve Turner*	102
Harvey	*Judith Viorst*	106
Best Friends	*Marian Swinger*	107
Not Just You, Me as Well	*David Harmer*	108
Gwyneth's Book of Records	*Mike Johnson*	110
Cefn Coed	*Robin Mellor*	112
Holidays	*Pie Corbett*	114
Best Friend	*Roger Stevens*	116

And Childhood Was Mine . . .

Long, Long Ago	*Clive Webster*	120
Aunt Sue's Stories	*Langston Hughes*	121
Houses	*Robert Hull*	123
At Cider Mill Farm	*David Harmer*	125
Salford Road	*Gareth Owen*	127

In a Grandmother's House – Glasgow, 1960	*John Rice*	130
The Family Book	*Brian Moses*	133
Ancestors	*Edward Braithwaite*	134
The Picnic in Jammu	*Zulfikar Ghose*	137
And Even Now	*Dorothy Livesay*	139
The Wolf Next Door But One	*Paul Cookson*	140
My First Dog	*Patricia Leighton*	142
Summer's End	*Doris Corti*	144
At the End of the Second World War	*Wes Magee*	146
My Ship	*Christy Brown*	148
How Do You Say Goodbye?	*Lois Simmie*	149

Trust Your Dreams

Dreamtime	*Judith Nicholls*	152
Pegasus	*Clare Bevan*	153
A Small Dragon	*Brian Patten*	154
They Don't Know Everything	*Roger Stevens*	156
Romance	*Walter James Turner*	158
Dream of a Bird	*Bach Nga Thi Tran*	160
A Feather from an Angel	*Brian Moses*	162
Poem for Kids	*John Wain*	164
Dreaming the Unicorn	*Tony Mitton*	170
To You	*Langston Hughes*	172

I Remember, I Remember

I remember, I remember,
The house where I was born,
The little window where the sun
Came peeping in at morn;
He never came a wink too soon,
Nor brought too long a day,
But now I often wish the night
Had borne my breath away.

I remember, I remember,
The roses, red and white;
The violets, and the lily-cups,
Those flowers made of light!
The lilacs where the robin built,
And where my brother set
The laburnum on his birthday –
The tree is living yet!

I remember, I remember,
Where I was used to swing;
And thought the air must rush as fresh
To swallows on the wing:
My spirit flew in feathers then,
That is so heavy now,
And summer pools could hardly cool
The fever on my brow!

I remember, I remember,
The fir trees dark and high;
I used to think their slender tops
Were close against the sky:
It was a childish ignorance
But now 'tis little joy
To know I'm farther off from Heav'n
Than when I was a boy.

Thomas Hood

A Place Without Footprints

Do We Know?

Do we know
where this boat is going
as we float between the stars? –

As we tell old tales
spun with moon-webs and mysteries
and drink darkness
from tall twisting jars?

As we swirl in strange circles
tracked by lost winds and dolphins,
who is leading us on?
And do *they* even know
where this journey will take us,
from midnight to starlight to dawn?

David Greygoose

Going Down

In a cool green rush
     we hurtle
          down
through a tunnel of pine
lush perfumed darkness
bicycle wheels erasing
the slow slog up

we leave everything –
even our grins
race after us now

in a trail of amazement . . .

Helen Lamb

The Special Place

It was my special place,
My secret, my safety.
The day the bully picked on me,
The day the rabbit died,
The day the teacher said I was a cheat,
I went there, to my special place.

> A mossy boulder I could climb,
> A tiny, bubbling waterfall,
> A little pond to paddle in,
> Mysterious as a black pearl.

I went back ten years later,
And took my brother,
The day he started school.
But when I looked, and looked again.
My special place had gone,
Bewitched by some bad magic.

> A lumpish rock, too small to climb,
> A little, trickling water-spout,
> A muddy pool, all overgrown,
> Grim and grey as old dust.

But then I saw my brother's face
And it was shining.
'Brilliant!' he said. 'I think it's brill,
Our special place.'

Jennifer Curry

If Once You have Slept on an Island

If once you have slept on an island
  You'll never be quite the same;
You may look as you looked the day before
  And go by the same old name,

You may bustle about in street and shop;
  You may sit at home and sew,
But you'll see blue water and wheeling gulls
  Wherever your feet may go.

You may chat with the neighbours of this and that
  And close to your fire keep,
But you'll hear ship whistle and lighthouse bell
  And tides beat through your sleep.

Oh, you won't know why, and you can't say how
    Such change upon you came,
But – once you have slept on an island
    You'll never be quite the same!

Rachel Field

The Shining

That day when I was on the shore,
out further than I'd been before
I found a place all to myself
closed in by rocks and cliff,
where the only sound was lapping water
my steps, the seagull's laughter.

Hard sand and rocks went shelving steep
into clear water, cold and deep . . .
and deeper, darker, pure and still.
The sky was grey, the air was chill –
it seemed the same as it would be
with nobody on earth to see.

This was the kind of hidden nook
where you find treasure – in one look,
millions of pebbles, smooth and round
from age on age of being ground
against each other, to make them shine,
waiting for me to make them mine.

But seemed like something not to touch
in a museum or empty church,
kept from everyone, under glass,
beauties, set inside their case,
glistening with every colour
each one different from each other.

I had to take one – some – to keep –
but the moment each was in my grip
they changed to mere wet weights of stone,
everything I wanted – gone –
faded – damp, pale, grey, and dry.
It was enough to make you cry.

Just one came home with me, that still
sits in the dust on my window sill;
and though they say, just throw it out,
I remember the shining of it,
and wonder, what other things might shine
and still be mine, and still be mine.

Brian Lee

Boy on the Beach

Walking the dunes
Behind the strand,
I saw a boy alone
On wide, wet sand.
A stillness held him
As he faced the tide,
Slowly raised his arms
Then spread them wide;
Stayed so for a minute
Then, breaking the spell,
Wrote large on the sand
With a stone or shell.
Walking on through marram grass
I soon could see:
He'd simply written,
I AM ME.

Eric Finney

Midsummer Magic

We climbed the hill
(Mum, Dad, Josie and me)
humping travel rug, thermos flask, torch,
our pockets crammed with chocolate bars.

Up we went through bilberry tracks,
stubbing toes on rocks as hunched
and shoulder-slouched
as sleeping down-and-outs.
Small paws scurried unseen
in the unreal half-light which
swung between night and day
and the odd Midsummer star
hung on.

Panting, our breaths making
small breezes, we reached the top;
saw Herefordshire, a grey quilt
stitched by ghost hedges,
spread far below.
No talking, said Dad,
Not a whisper, said Mum
Just sit – and wait.
So –

        chewing soft chocolate
        and sipping hot tea
                – we did.

Cool winds brushed our cheeks,
flurried the tufty grass; earth smells
and heather smells filled our heads
and then . . .
        the horizon beat like a pulse,
grey lightened to white, to silver, pale gold.
The sun rose, lit the sky with its rays,
threw primrose yellow
over a silent world.

We watched as fields greened,
gates and gables glowed, and tiny
jet and pearl cattle stirred to graze;
we gasped at the glimmering square
of upside-down linseed sky
over by Parker's Farm.
And halfway down the hill
in the topmost branch
of a rowan tree
a blackbird burst into song.

Patricia Leighton

In the Moonlight

We looked out of our bedroom at moonlight:
Now how could we go to sleep
When the world out there was as bright as day
And the snow was lying deep?

So we muffled up and out we went –
Nobody heard us go –
And we stood in the magic of moonlight
In a garden wrapped in snow.

Everything changed, enchanted:
Our garden seat a throne,
The bushes softly smothered,
The trees as white as bone.

For a while we could only look,
Held in a spell, but soon
We were shaping hard, cold snowballs
And throwing them at the moon.

Tomorrow: snowmen and snowfights
And clearing a track for the cars,
Treading it all into slush, but tonight
We snowballed the moon and stars.

Eric Finney

Home

It was only a box
on an edge of town estate
which even to me at ten
looked small and thin walled
in its bare and tiny garden.

But we would be the first
to live here
which meant
this house would be haunted
by no other family's ghosts.

And the moment I stepped
through its sunny door
and heard its whispered promise
I felt such a glow of pleasure
that I knew this would be
the warmest of friendships.

Philip Waddell

Until We Built a Cabin

When we lived in a city
(three flights up and down)
I never dreamed how many stars
could show above a town.

When we moved to a village
where lighted streets were few,
I thought I could see all the stars,
But, oh, I never knew –

Until we built a cabin
where hills are high and far,
I never knew how many
                    many
                        stars there really are!

Aileen Fisher

The Shooting Stars

That night
we went out in the dark
and gazed up at the sky
and saw the shooting stars
was one of the best nights ever

It was as if someone
was throwing paint
across the universe

And the stars kept coming
and we 'oohed' and 'aahed'
like on bonfire night

And it didn't matter
they weren't real stars –
just bits of dust on fire
burning up in the atmosphere

And we stayed out there for ages
standing on this tiny planet
staring up at the vast cosmos

And I shivered
with the thrill
of it all

James Carter

A Place without Footprints

I'm searching for a place
Without footprints,
But I'm the youngest child.

Whatever I try,
Wherever I go,
Whatever I choose,
One of them has already
Succeeded,
Been there,
Chosen first.
I'm just a comparison,
Usually unfavourable.
Born to follow,
To repeat the pattern,
The footprints are never mine.

But I'll keep moving,
Hoping the direction is new,
Hoping that one day
A space *will* appear
Like a fresh snowfall,
Untouched,
Unnoticed by the others,
As I'm searching for a place
Without footprints,
As I'm searching for a place
To plant mine.

Daphne Kitching

The Music of Dripping Stones

The Well

I found a well once
In the dark green heart of a wood

Where pigeons ruffled up into a skylight of branches
And disappeared.

The well was old, so mossed and broken
It was almost a part of the wood

Gone back to nature. Carefully, almost fearfully,
I looked down into its depths

And saw the lip of water shifting and tilting,
Heard the music of dripping stones.

I stretched down, cupped a deep handful
Out of the winter darkness of its world

And drank. That water tasted of moss, of secrets,
Of ancient meetings, of laughter,

Of dark stone, of crystal –
It reached the roots of my being

Assuaged a whole summer of thirst.
I have been looking for that water ever since.

Kenneth C. Steven

Mapping Our World

The stream. Our special place,
In a tangle of woods
At the edge of the park.
It flowed through our childhood,
Ripple-voiced, light-darting,
With minnows in the shallows,
Mind-monsters in the deeps.
We followed it, mapped it,
Named its broads and narrows,
Its dams, falls and pools,
Waded, splashed, climbed, fished,
Knew the deep slow places under trees,
The soft mud that sucked at our legs,
The small Niagara where leaves rode the rapids,
The creaking branch, a bridge
For teetering tightrope-walkers,
The spangled green moss-cushion,
The lurking crocodile log.
We knew that scattered acorn-cups
Held drinks for fairies,
And that hazelnuts
Were nibbled by tiny teeth.

We knew the magic there
Would shimmer and dazzle
If only we could come by moonlight,
To see what crept from the mudbank
Abseiled from the trees
And danced in the shallows
Enchanting the fish.

While we whispered plans and secrets
The grown-ups shared flasks and gossip.
Answering their call, we came at last
Across the grass, wild with adventure,
Mud-streaked, moss-flecked, twig-snagged,
Story-mazed, stream-charmed,
And pitied them –

For their world
So much smaller than ours.

Linda Newbery

The Tunnel

This is the way that I have to go
I've left all my friends behind
back there, where a faint light glimmers
round the long tunnel's bend.

I can't see a roof up above me,
I can't find either wall,
My shoes slip on the slimy boulders –
How deep is it down, if I fall?

Beneath me the same stream flows
that laughed in the fields back there –
Here, it is black, with the leeches and weeds,
and the bats flitting through the dank air.

It's just the same if I shut my eyes:
my companions, all around,
are trickles, drips, sploshes, sudden *plops*,
and that strange, sucking sound.

One shoe's full of the cold dark water,
my hands slither over the stones,
my throat's gone dry, my heart pound-pounds,
but I can only go on –

till I can see them, they can see me,
and again they start to shout,
The rats bite, watch out for the rats,
but now I am almost out:

dizzy, happy, I blink at the light,
The sun still shines, the birds still sing.
Someone is patting me on the back –
Now I am one of the gang.

Brian Lee

Summer in Brooklyn

Fortune
> has its cookies to give out

which is a good thing

> since it's been a long time since

that summer in Brooklyn
when they closed off the street
> one hot day
> and the

                    FIREMEN
> turned on their hoses
and all the kids ran out in it

> in the middle of the street

and there were

> maybe a couple dozen of us
>> out there
with the water squirting up
> to the

                     sky
                             and all over
                                                us
there was maybe only six of us
                                      kids altogether
                running around in our
                                  barefeet and birthday
        suits
                and I remember Molly but then
the firemen stopped squirting their hoses
                        all of a sudden and went
                                        back in
                                their firehouse
                                        and
            started playing pinochle again
                    just as if nothing
                        had ever
                                        happened
while I remember Molly
                        looked at me and

        ran in

because I guess really we were the only ones there

                                Lawrence Ferlinghetti

The Old Canal

On the stillest of still days
We lay on the towpath to look
Down into clear depths.
We saw ourselves looking up, drowned.
We tapped the water with fingertips
And our faces wobbled like jelly.
Tapped again and they broke up.

Under the bridge, cool and dark:
Light bounced off deep water
To play on the bridging vault
Of curving brick: a ghostly
Play of wavy trembling light,
Oscillating, oscillating.

Every day, the dare:
To cross the bridge, outside the wall.
A bare toe-hold on the lip of bricks.
Clung to the parapet, arms outstretched.
Fingers aching, scratching a hold.
Reached safety, trembling.

Near factories, canal-water
Always a rusty red soup,
Stinking of bitter iron.
We threw sticks: 'Fetch it, boy!'
He did, and stank to high heaven
For at least a week.
'Stay outside, pongy dog!'

Old sacks, stacked with bricks,
Took dead dogs to the bottom,
Lay in deep mud, disintegrated.
The corpses rose, ballooned,
The colours of death.

In clear stretches, stickle-
Backs, big-eyed, flickery.
We netted them, scraped off
The limpets, little plates
Like cancers: gristly
Grizzled and grisly.

Water boatmen, long-legged,
Balanced on dimples of water,
Performing their ordinary miracle.
Dragonflies, encased in enamel,
Decorated the flags with their pennants.

Beetles, shoe-black shiny,
Shot up like rockets,
Surfaced, gulped air,
Then down again
Like suicidal dive-bombers.

Best of all, the barge-horses,
Thudding, treading
For purchase, straining
Shouldering, muscles at a stretch.

Ropes of grassy saliva
Hung, swinging.
And the barge, dark as night,
Looming like a giant coffin.
Always at the stern, silent,
A man or woman at the tiller,
Dark and silent as an undertaker.

Worst of all, my brother getting lost.
We searched the towpaths, bridges.
Was he already under water?
At ten, he couldn't swim,
Was crazy about canals.

At nightfall, he was still not found.
Fears bubbled up
Inside our minds,
Like the frantic gurgling
Of a drowning boy.

His face was in my mind's eye,
White, silent, staring from eyes
Now blind, wide open, dead.

When he came strolling home,
A torrent of questions.
'What's all the fuss about?'
He asked. He'd found
A new exciting friend
With an even more exciting,
Even newer model railway.
Shunting, moving signals,
Changing points,
They'd lost all track of time.

He was sent upstairs.
Then thrashed.
There was a sudden rush
Of sheer vexation,
The sharp anger of relief.
For months, every night,
Falling asleep I saw
His drowning face.

Geoffrey Summerfield

Heatwave Summer

The summer I was nine
I grew
A white skin bikini
With brown arms and legs
My nose peeled
And I wore
White sand stockings on my wet legs.
Got water up my nose
And sand in the sheets.
Went up and down escalators
(With sore feet)
And tried on a hundred black school shoes all size
one-and-a-half
Ate ice-blocks at teatime
(And grew a pink moustache)
Ate fish and chips in paper.
Kissed half-forgotten uncles
And danced in tingling seas
In a holiday heatwave.

Cathy Warry

Being Late

Sometimes we'd watch it chug away,
The red bus to school,
Even wave it goodbye,
As it plunged over the dip
And vanished.

Being late didn't seem to matter much.
It was summer.
We could scuff our shoes,
Hurl bags high over the hedges,
Stare at pigs,
Stick poppies behind our ears.

All morning
We had the ambling lanes,
Footpaths, streams,
Cows, corn,
Poppies.

We could track the ice-cream van,
Pitching and rolling along the trail,
Make it stop,
Deliver up
Raspberry Ripples.

We could zigzag our way
Up Old Beau hill,
Gasp, squeal,
Turn and wave,
Watch poppies waving back.

Then,
Pulling faces,
Practising excuses,
Zoom down the last lap,
Wings out like planes.

Mary Green

Going

Crossing alone
the dark glassy surface
of the lake among the trees
where no one else is;
I drift, halfway
between the rotting boathouse
and the hidden landing stage
sinking in the sedge
that shifts and whispers
although there is no breeze.
A pale heron stands
still, on one leg, to watch
my slow ragged row
in the heavy boat I borrow
each time I'm here:
my hollow *thuds* and splashes sink
deep into the black
woods that go up steep
and topple into sky –
no sound of me comes back.
Alone, I hardly spoil
this motionless expanse

at all; as if oil
were what I slid across
my slow progressions close
up behind me,
instantaneous.

Where I am now
now, is a moment ago,
a memory I may
forget, myself, one day . . .
Between what comes and goes
or stays, or moves
there is an edge that is
always, here and now,
finer than a knife,
cutting into my life,
and making it my own:
the future flows
into me, and through
and instantly renews,
as underneath the prow,
clear, continuous,

the waters stay, but go,
still, but slipping past,
as they move, or I move,
going, slow or fast,
reflecting sky and sedge,
deeps, below, above,
and, in between them, I,
on my way, here and now,
in an eternity,
out, always, on time's edge.

Brian Lee

By St Thomas Water

By St Thomas Water
Where the river is thin
We looked for a jam-jar
To catch the quick fish in.
Through St Thomas Churchyard
Jessie and I ran
The day we took the jam-pot
Off the dead man.

On the scuffed tombstone
The grey flowers fell,
Cracked was the water,
Silent the shell.
The snake for an emblem
Swirled on the slab,
Across the beach of sky the sun
Crawled like a crab.

'If we walk,' said Jessie,
'Seven times round,
We shall hear a dead man
Speaking underground.'
Round the stone we danced, we sang,
Watched the sun drop,
Laid our heads and listened
At the tomb-top.

Soft as the thunder
At the storm's start
I heard a voice as clear as blood,
Strong as the heart.
But what words were spoken
I can never say,
I shut my fingers round my head,
Drove them away.

'What are those letters, Jessie,
Cut so sharp and trim
All round this holy stone
With earth up to the brim?'
Jessie traced the letters
Black as coffin-lead.
'He is not dead but sleeping,'
Slowly she said.

I looked at Jessie,
Jessie looked at me,
And our eyes in wonder
Grew wide as the sea.
Past the green and bending stones
We fled hand in hand,
Silent through the tongues of grass
To the river strand.

By the creaking cypress
We moved as soft as smoke
For fear all the people
Underneath awoke.
Over all the sleepers
We darted light as snow
In case they opened up their eyes,
Called up from below.

Many a day has faltered
Into many a year
Since the dead awoke and spoke
And we would not hear.
Waiting in the cold grass
Under a crinkled bough,
Quiet stone, cautious stone,
What do you tell me now?

Charles Causley

Ice

was the first time
anyone remembers it happening

the fields froze
in our village
in south china

we broke some
not knowing what it was
and took it to the junk peddler

he thought it was glass
and traded us a penny
for it

he wrapped it up
in old cloth and placed it
on top of his basket

of course
the noonday sun melted it

by the time
we came back with more
he had gotten wise

Jim Wong-Chu

Such a World Comes In

Doing Nothing Much

I could potter for hours on a lonely beach
Picking pebbles to roll in my hand,
Wondering where will the next wave reach,
Writing my name in the sand.

Near the tumbling weir, where the hawthorn's pink,
I could sit for hours in a trance
Watching the water stream to the brink
And the white foam pound and dance.

Or high on a headland find me,
While a seagull wheels and dips,
Gazing for hours out to sea
At islands and smudges of ships.

Eric Finney

Dad's Shed

is

a shadow-place
of spiders,

dusty, cobwebby,
smelling of rust,

sawdust, glue
and oily rags;

bits of metal,
things forever

half-fixed, unfixed,
unmended;

jars of nails, screws,
and rock-hard

paintbrushes
a million years old:

a sort of secret place
only my dad

and the spiders
understand.

Matt Simpson

Den to Let

To let
One self-contained
Detached den.
Accommodation is compact
Measuring one yard square.
Ideal for two eight-year-olds
Plus one small dog
Or two cats
Or six gerbils.
Accommodation consists of
One living room
Which doubles as a kitchen
Bedroom
Entrance-hall
Dining room
Dungeon
Space capsule
Pirate boat
Covered wagon
Racing car
Palace
Aeroplane

Junk room
And lookout post.
Property is southward facing
And can be found
Within a short walking distance
Of the back door
At bottom of garden.
Easily found in the dark
By following the smell
Of old cabbages and tea bags.
Convenient escape routes
Past rubbish dump
To Seager's Lane
Through hole in hedge,
Or into next door's garden;
But beware of next door's rhinoceros
Who sometimes thinks he's a poodle.
Construction is of
Sound corrugated iron
And roof doubles as shower
During rainy weather.
Being partially underground,
Den makes
A particularly effective hiding place

When in a state of war
With older sisters
Brothers
Angry neighbours
Or when you simply want to be alone.
Some repair work needed
To north wall
Where Mr Spence's foot came through
When planting turnips last Thursday.
With den go all contents
Including:
One carpet – very smelly
One teapot – cracked
One woolly penguin –
No beak and only one wing
One unopened tin
Of sultana pud
One hundred and three *Beanos*
Dated 1983–1985
And four *Rupert* annuals
Rent is free
The only payment being
That the new occupant
Should care for the den

In the manner to which it has been accustomed
And on long summer evenings
     Heroic songs of days gone by
     Should be loudly sung
     So that old and glorious days
     Will never be forgotten.

Gareth Owen

Once Upon a Time and Space

Grandpa had an
ancient telescope,
poked out of
his garden shed.
'Let's go
harvesting tonight
and gather a
bouquet of stars.'

Secrets of time and space
were his allotment,
burgeoning with
petals of light
known as:
Orion
Ursa Major
Cassiopeia,
each flower complete
with its own myth.

Hours we sat. As his
thermos flask emptied,
'giant Jupiter'
blazed brightly
and, close to midnight,
he told me all about
'mysterious Mars'.

Most brilliant blossom of all,
Grandpa's 'man in the moon'
still blooms,
to smile on secret dreams.

Goodnight, Grandpa.

Mike Johnson

The Christmas Shed

It was late afternoon on Christmas Day
with light fading and flakes falling
when the three of us raced through the copse
where rhododendrons and holly bushes
bent low under their burden of fresh snow.
Gasping, we skidded to a stop
at the edge of the estate's allotments.
A bitter, whining wind made us shiver
as it whipped across the frozen earth.
          'No one's about. Come on!'

Slipping and skating we dashed to Jacko's shed
and at the back crawled in through a hole
where the old boards had rotted away.
Inside it was dry. The air was still.
We peered as daylight filtered dimly
through the fly-spattered, cobwebby window,
and breathed the shed's special smell
of pine, creosote, paraffin and sawdust.
Fear of discovery made us whisper.
          'Let's see if they're there.'

Carefully we moved garden implements
that were stacked in a corner.
Dried soil fell and crunched beneath our boots
as we shifted rakes, forks, spades and hoes,
and there was Smoky and her four kittens,
warm in a bed of worn gloves and jerseys.
Like the Three Kings we knelt and offered
our Christmas gifts – turkey scraps, ham, a sausage.
Smoky arched and purred and ate hungrily.
        'The kittens are still blind.'

The food vanished. We watched in silence
as the grey cat lay down and her mewling kittens
guzzled greedily at the milk bar.
'It's late.' We replaced the implements
and crept out of Jacko's old shed.
Like shadows we hared for the cover of the copse.
Now the snow was heavy. Day's last light was dying.
Chilled to the bone we reached our estate
where Christmas lights were flashing. We split.
        'Same time tomorrow?'
                'Yeah.'
                        'See you.'

Wes Magee

Singing in the Streets

I had almost forgotten the singing in the streets,
Snow piled up by the houses, drifting
Underneath the door into the warm room.
Firelight, lamplight, the little lame cat
Dreaming in soft sleep on the hearth, mother
   dozing.
Waiting for Christmas to come, the boys and me
Trudging over blanket fields waving lanterns to
   the sky.
I had almost forgotten the smell, the feel of it
   all,
The coming back home, with girls laughing like
   stars,
Their cheeks, holly berries, me kissing one,
Silent-tongued, soberly, by the long church wall;
Then back to the kitchen table, supper on the
   white cloth.
Cheese, bread, the home-made wine,
Symbols of the night's joys, a holy feast.
And I wonder now, years gone, mother gone,
The boys and girls scattered, drifted away with
   the snowflakes,

Lamplight done, firelight over,
If the sounds of our singing in the streets are still
   there.
Those old tunes, still praising;
And now, a lifetime of Decembers away from it
   all,
A branch of remembering holly stabs my cheeks,
And I think it may be so;
Yes, I believe it may be so.

James Reeves

Snow Spell

This is our summer place

But the trees are bare
and all the leaves are crisp
and the river that we paddled in,
is slow and clinks with ice.
The air smokes from us
our voices echo thin and sharp as sleet
and everything is sleeping under snow

In summer we were playing here,
we built a dam,
my skimmer bounced in six times
a wet dog ate our sandwiches,
and Dad fell off the stepping stones
you swam your first five strokes.
The air was full of barks and laughs and shouts.

Not long ago, before the spell of snow.

Berlie Doherty

Requiem for a Robin

Our mother let us deal with it ourselves.
She swore she'd never have another cat.
We chose a spot beneath the apple tree
Directly underneath the branch he sat
And carolled on. We thought he would approve.
It's hard to say exactly how it felt
To take a spade and dig our friend a grave.
We smoothed his feathers down and then I knelt
To place him in the ground. He looked so small
Compared to when he overflowed with song.
I shuddered when I covered him with earth
And hoped his mate would not grieve for too
   long.
We sang no hymns, but knew he would be heard
Where lamb lies down with lion, cat with bird.

Sue Cowling

from *Growing Up Alone*

At Cheerio Point me and Sandy
knew a place where

we'd go behind the tree sometimes
and stare into the eyes of God

they were in the face
of an old yellow cat who'd gone mad

once we had looked
we wouldn't be able to move

sometimes we'd have to sit there
for hours waiting

before it let us go

Robert Adamson

The Magic of the Brain

Such a sight I saw:
An eight-sided kite surging up into a cloud
Its eight tails streaming out as if they were one.
It lifted my heart as starlight lifts the head
Such a sight I saw.

And such a sound I heard.
One bird through dim winter light as the day was
   closing
Poured out a song suddenly from an empty tree.
It cleared my head as water refreshes the skin
Such a sound I heard.

Such a smell I smelled:
A mixture of roses and coffee, of green leaf and
   warmth.
It took me to gardens and summer and cities abroad,
Memories of meetings as if my past friends were here
Such a smell I smelled.

Such soft fur I felt.
It wrapped me around, soothing my winter-cracked
  skin,
Not gritty or stringy or sweaty but silkily warm
As my animal slept on my lap, and we both breathed
  content
Such soft fur I felt.

Such food I tasted:
Smooth-on-tongue soup, and juicy crackling of meat,
Greens like fresh fields, sweet-on-your-palate peas,
Jellies and puddings with fragrance of fruit they are
  made from
Such good food I tasted:

Such a world comes in:
Far world of the sky to breathe in through your nose
Near world you feel underfoot as you walk on the
    land.
Through your eyes and your ears and your mouth
    and your brilliant brain
Such a world comes in.

Jenny Joseph

The White Ball
Never Fell . . .

My Old Jumper

Putting on my old jumper
Is an adventure.
It has so many holes
That you never know
Where
Your arms are going to end up.

John Coldwell

Street Cricket

On August evenings by the lamp-post
When the days are long and light
The lads come out for cricket
And play until it's night.
They bat and bowl and field and shout
And someone shouts 'HOWZAT!'
But you can't give Peter Batty out
Or he'll take away his bat.

The dogs in the Close all love to field
And chase about the street
The stumper wears his mother's gloves
And stops the ball with his feet.
Everyone should have a bowl
That's the proper way to play
But Batty has to bowl all night
Or he takes his ball away.

When lamps and rooms turn on their lights
And you can hardly see the ball
The lads begin to drift off home
You can hear the goodbyes they call.
But Peter Batty's two hundred not out
And he shouts as he walks away,
'Remember I'm batting tomorrow night
Or I won't let anyone play.'

Gareth Owen

A Better Game

Down our no-through road the game
Was football and of course
We played it every day. Our house
Blocked off the traffic at one end,
Which made life safer, though they told us
Watch out and be careful and the sign
They'd put there, well to say the least
It didn't always work. But that
Was fair enough because you really can
Get tired of football, and we did,
And that was when we went in
For a drink, a spot of telly, then
Came out to settle on the doorstep
Waiting for a misdirected car
Or angry truck to cruise or trundle
Helplessly towards us, as a face
Began to fill the windscreen

Tight-lipped, baffled behind glass
And uninvited, slowly, slowly
Rolling into earshot just
Too late for turning back
Before our cheery, wicked waving
Changed to laughter and *Dead End!*
Dead End! we chanted, louder,
Louder, as an even better game than football
Ended in a victory for us.

John Mole

Hill Rolling

I kind of exploded inside,
and joy shot out of me.
I began my roll down the grassy hill.
I bent my knees up small, took a deep breath
And I was off.
My arms shot out sideways.
I gathered speed.
My eyes squinted.
Sky and grass, dazzle and dark.

I went on for ever,
My arms were covered with dents,
holes, squashed grass.
Before I knew it I was at the bottom.
The game was over.
The door of the classroom closed behind me.
I can smell chalk dust, and hear the voice of
    teacher,
to make me forget my hill

Andrew Taylor

Conker Crazy

Once a year
the craze came round –
we'd chuck sticks
into the big conker tree
by Samways Lane
and scrabble for
king-sized prizes.
'Iddy, iddy onker,
my first conker.
Iddy, iddy ack,
my first whack,'
we'd chant.
Taking a crack
on the knuckles
was part of the game.
Each breaktime
we'd gather by the sheds
to try to make
our chosen conker
up to a 'tenner' –
Some talked of
stewed conkers

dipped in vinegar,
others buried them
till they turned black.
My friend Donald
told stories of a King conker,
an invincible ace,
that his dad had owned.
Too often I'd end up
with tangled strings
or halves in the gutter.
On the way back home
I'd mutter to my brothers
of a dream conker,
hard as concrete,
that I'd stash away
for a year or two.
Then I'd return,
conker crazy,
to St Peters Primary
ready to take my revenge.

Pie Corbett

Fishing Summer

Michael and I were fishing companions
rushing to catch the tide before it turned,
our tackle spilling from saddlebags, our
pockets crammed with fat paper wallets of
fresh dug lug. And casting we'd encounter
familiar hazards, reels span at our first
attempts, lines tangled and sprouted birds' nests;
we spent precious time unravelling till
tides turned and the fish bit fast. We caught an
old lag of a crab that came up fighting:
It bubbled and spat with vicious claws splayed
out like a baseball catcher, then edged off
sideways across the pier to drop-plop down
to water beneath. There were rumours too
of some dreadful beasts that slithered from clefts
in search of food, of monster congers that
wrapped their tails round rocks and then gave
    battle.
There were times when we wished the big fish
    would
bite, though we doubted the strength of our
    lines.

We'd visualize fantastic catches,
our photos in angling magazines, but
nothing that size ever gobbled our bait.

Michael and I were fishing companions
packing away with the last of the light
before slinking home along alleyways
while darkness spread its nets all over town.

Brian Moses

The Ascent of Everest

On the last afternoon of the holidays
We three intrepid mountaineers
Climbed Everest – again;

We'd already done it in the morning.

But, this time by the most difficult route,
Across the South Ridge
And up the treacherous North Face;

The side by the banisters.

Once again, Chris Bonnington (that's me)
Little Jack and Samantha our faithful guide,
Struggled across the endless foothills;

By the telephone table.

Then huddled together, we stood staring up
Through the late afternoon mists,
At the fearful white cliff;

Of the upstairs toilet door.

And so we set off up the Great Glacier.
Pausing only once, flat against the ice wall,
To let another solitary mountaineer squeeze by;

To get to the loo.

Then at last – halfway up – Camp 6,
We stopped nearly exhausted;
Just long enough to catch our breath;

And eat our smoky-bacon crisps and Smarties.

Then on, climbing, climbing ever upwards,
For the final assault on the summit.
At last, we stood on the roof of the world;

Up there by the landing radiator.

Hugs and handshakes all round,
And three hearty cheers.
Then, it was Samantha's turn to plant the flag;

In the vase on the window sill.

Then down, down, the icy slopes.
A brief stop at Camp 6 to collect our litter.
Finally, on to base camp, civilization and;

Into the kitchen for Coke, Kit-Kats and – Kathmandu

David Whitehead

Little Houses

Houses I have made and loved:
three umbrellas in the garden
a blanket on the floor
make a pavilion for one princess.

A draped sheet, a clothes horse
become a ridge tent
hideaway on rainy days,
camping in the house.

Bigger houses take longer.
One we lived in for three days,
and even kept the rain out,
boasted a corrugated-iron roof.

There were three rooms,
mattresses on the floor.
At night our mothers
wondered who we were.

Angela Topping

The Magical Bicycle

My best surprise
Was my shining bike
With its silver voice
But I couldn't ride it.

Every time I tried it
threw me off.
I think it thought
It was a horse.

I bruised my knees.
I banged my chin.
I tried again, again, again.

My brother can glide it
round and round
Jenny can race it up and down
Even my uncle can wobble astride it
Everybody I know can ride it.
It must be something to do with magic,
There must be a special, secret trick.
There must be a spell on bikes, I decided.

Dad ran up the entry, holding on
and then he ran all the way down
and panted all the way up again.

'Just turn your legs!'
He grew tired and slow.
'You won't fall off.'

and I never did
Till he let go.

But every night, deep in my dreams
I rode my bike
over the trees,
as high as the birds,
over the mountains
over the world.
And every day I tried again.
I gave my dad another chance
'I WILL ride my bike!' I shouted out loud.
And I fell off.

I spat on my hands
And rubbed my knees
I picked up my bike
and tried to look proud.

'It's just a matter of magic,' I said.
'That's all it is.'
Isn't it?

And one day,
I must have
said it.
The magic word.
I didn't hear it.
Or think it.
It must have been
in a quiet bit of my mind.

There was Dad, running behind me.
I could hear his footsteps
getting fainter and fainter,
and I could feel the air
on my face and in my hair,
I could feel my own power
I could feel my own strength
I could hear the wheels turning
My legs were like pistons
And I knew I could do it
I could cycle for ever.

Like a bird over mountains
Like a ship over oceans
To the end of the world
I had magic in me.

Berlie Doherty

Paradise

Climbing up into my father's
Barrow of cut grass
And sinking gently, all that
Thick warm moisture
Moulded round me, then
The mower's hum becoming louder,
Nearer, stuttering to a halt
And Dad pretending not to know
I'm in there, shaking out
Another load of luscious
Freshness on to me and muttering,
I wonder where he is?
And me about to answer,
Here I am, but then
Deciding not to.

John Mole

Hiding Places

While she counts to a hundred
through a veil of fingers

you are breathing red velvet
behind the stairway curtain
soaking up living-room murmurs of aunts
pretending they don't know where you are.

Or you are crouching behind Dad's shed
among water-butt toads and stinky compost,
mossy window frames and waving branches
outstaring next door's ever curious cat.

Or you are squeezing between heavy-scented lilac
and your playhouse window
trying not to give the game away
with your reflection in the glass.

Or you are flattening against the house wall,
beyond where a chimney breast juts out,
fingers reddening with brick dust,
risking the sudden hellos of nosy neighbours.

Or you are scrunching inside the airing cupboard
arms tight round the water tank
stifling giggles and whispers
among warm fluff and watery gurgles.

Or you are curling under the spare bed
in space the Hoover never reaches
among lost toys and magazines,
dolls' legs and silent dust.

You must not move
even though your nose is tickling,
your foot is itching,
your breath is trembling.

Any minute now
she could come creeping
near
nearer
and find you.

Sue Dymoke

Well Hidden

This is where I was when searching voices were
   calling me.
I was in places where time had no meaning;
among tangled tall grass within the rough walls
of the roofless ropewalks that stretched to the
   braehead,
watching huge snails wander through broken
   pantiles
under a sky aching with distance and the
   seagull's cry;
am I there? or am I in the shed whose windows
   are dark with dust,
whose warped benches and clay pots are coated
   with dust, that smells
of this dust of dry earth and the wood's slow rot,
of the green skin on the rainbarrel and oil in a
   rusting can,
where everything has been holding its breath for
   a long time
and vaguely stirs as I potter round and goes back
   to its secret dreaming
when I leave. For I am not there. I am upstairs in
   a room squeezed

into the slope of the roof, a room whose door is
  disguised as a cupboard,
whose walls are pasted with newspapers as old
  as my great-aunt,
only slightly yellowed where the weak light falls
  across the clutter
of long-locked trunks and suitcases stuffed with
  mothballed clothes,
and there I am sitting while the rain patters on
  the grimy skylight
reading of ferocious battles, sunk fishing boats
  and farm shows,
but do not think you can reach me there,
for they are all in the past, in my mind only,
and when I hide in them now, no one can find
  me.

Dave Calder

Game's End

On autumn evenings the children still play in the park,
Scuffing up the sweet-smelling aftermath,
Their shadows in the sunset triple length,
Making heroic kicks, half-legendary saves:
They play until it is dark,
And still for a little while after can be seen
By the flitting of their plimsolls, by their sleeves,
And by the twinkling orb of grass-stained polythene
Rising up white against dark sky or leaves.

Till, by some common consent, the game must close.
No one bothers any more to yell 'Pass' or 'Shoot',
Someone gives the ball a last terrific boot
Into the air and before it falls they are gone,
Wheeling away over the grass,
Snatching their sweaters up for the goalposts, going
Who knows where, only later to see how soon
The white ball never fell, but went on climbing
Into the dark air, and became the moon.

David Sutton

The Blue Marble

When I was a boy
I owned a marble.
Chipped it was
and pitted,
but when I looked inside,
one eye closed, the other
open wide to that
vista of blue light,
I thought it was a universe,
a world. It seemed so true,
could it be really there
inside that small glass globe
or in my head?
Wherever it was
I lost it.

Tony Mitton

If There is a
Train to Paradise

About Friends

The good thing about friends
is not having to finish sentences.

I sat a whole summer afternoon with my friend
    once
on a river bank, bashing heels on the baked mud
and watching the small chunks slide into the
    water
and listening to them – plop plop plop.
He said, 'I like the twigs when they . . . you
    know . . .
like that.' I said, 'There's that branch . . .'
We both said, 'Mmmm.' The river flowed and
    flowed
and there were lots of butterflies, that afternoon.

I first thought there was a sad thing about
    friends
when we met twenty years later.
We both talked hundreds of sentences,
taking care to finish all we said,
and explain it all very carefully,
as if we'd been discovered in places
we should not be, and were somehow ashamed.

I understood then what the river meant by
    flowing.

Brian Jones

Cranky, Scotty, Mooey and Me

We form a secret club,
Cranky, Scotty, Mooey and me,
with passwords
      secret signs
      membership
      a magazine
and a language
only we can understand.

We need a meeting place,
Cranky, Scotty, Mooey and me.
Cranky says a den
Scotty says a barn
I say a shed
and Mooey says
      a secret island
      surrounded by trees.

A secret island surrounded by trees!
A secret island surrounded by trees? say
Cranky, Scotty and me.
Yes, says Mooey
who draws a map of
      a field
      a wood
      a bridge
      and an island marked X.

Mooey's idea is voted on by
Cranky, Scotty, Mooey and me.
It wins 4–0.
It sounds just like
      William
      Treasure Island
      The Famous Five
      The Secret Seven.

The next weekend we meet up,
Cranky, Scotty, Mooey and me.
We hike over fields
      climb fences
      open gates
      skirt woods
      walk up hills
and then, below us, we see
the glint of water through leaves.
It's the secret lake
around the secret island.

We cut ourselves sticks to beat back the
    undergrowth,
Cranky, Scotty, Mooey and me.
Then it's right there in front of us
      with overhanging trees
      thick green rushes
      and a rickety wooden bridge.

At this point you expect something bad to
    happen to
Cranky, Scotty, Mooey and me.
Like, we all wake up and find that it's a dream
        the lake turns out to be a puddle
        the island is a molehill
        or the whole thing is a film set.

But it wasn't that way for
Cranky, Scotty, Mooey and me.
It was a real island
        in a real lake
        hidden in a real wood
and no one knew about it
        but us.

We sat in the bushes,
Cranky, Scotty, Mooey and me.
        listening to ducks
        watching gnats hit water
        thinking about treasure
wondering if life was always
this perfect.

Steve Turner

Harvey

Harvey doesn't laugh about how I stay short
   while everybody grows.
Harvey remembers I like jellybeans – except
   black.
Harvey lends me shirts I don't have to give
   back.
I'm scared of ghosts and only Harvey knows.

Harvey thinks I will when I say someday I will
   marry Margie Rose.
Harvey shares his lemonade – sip for sip.
He whispers 'zip' when I forget to zip.
He swears I don't have funny-looking toes.

Harvey calls me up when I'm in bed with a sore
   throat and runny nose.
Harvey says I'm nice – but not *too* nice.
And if there is a train to Paradise,
I won't get on it unless Harvey goes.

Judith Viorst

Best Friends

That's her.
The photo's a bit faded
but that's definitely her, my best friend Helen.
That's me beside her, the one with plaits.
Mum and Dad took us on a picnic that day.
We used to do everything together
and I remember saying,
'We'll be best friends for ever, won't we?'
Of course, we were only eight years old
and had yet to learn that nothing is for ever.

Marian Swinger

Not Just You, Me As Well

In the park they'd hang about
like giant birds of prey
jaws clamped around tough grins
eyes full of heavy punches.

I remember three of us
thrown down, our faces rubbed in mud
then rolled on our backs
gasping like three landed fish.

One sat hard on my chest
another stood there looking down
tapped my head with his shoe
said he didn't like me.

Time and time again it happened
in the park, at school, out playing
once I tried hitting back
they just hit me harder.

I suppose they've all grown up
manage banks, drive trucks, own shops
more unhappy now than ever
yelling at their wives and children.

They never learned to make us laugh
never learned to sing and dance
never learned to write a poem
never ever made a friend.

David Harmer

Gwyneth's Book of Records

I wonder what it's like to be
the cleverest person in the world?

Is it better to be tallest or smallest
or best to be the person
who's exactly in the middlest?

The loudest and the quietest
shouldn't live next door,
but would the strongest and the weakest
make good neighbours?
How about the slowest and the fastest?

The bravest person might be dad
or mum or daughter, brother, sister,
son of the kindest, tidiest
or funniest . . .

When I grow up I'm going to be
the happiest person in the world

and don't care if only I know I am.

Mike Johnson

Cefn Coed

*Cefn Coed is the psychiatric hospital
in Swansea, South Wales.*

Johnny's gone up Cefn Coed,
I miss seeing him along the road,
talking to stones and
singing his wordless songs.

We used to talk of sheep
and flowers, and the wild
things he did in his youth.

He would gaze happily across
the purple mist hills and
murmur about those long-lost
times that used to be.

He would tell me about
the time all Wales was saved
by his heroic act,
but never said what,

and how, in the war,
the shell landed so close
that it shaved seven men.

I used to see him on my way
down to swim in the north bays,
and wave to him in the
scarlet dusk, on my return,

and he would smile, pat dogs
and play marbles with
an invisible ball bearing.

The children will have no one
to run after now, and I
will have no one to talk to
about winds and seas and
things impossible.

                              Robin Mellor

Holidays

We never went
anywhere exotic –
best friends' parents picked
faraway places,
came back with sun-tanned faces
from Malaga and Malibu,
knew how to avoid jet lag.
Their bags labelled
with names that breathed magic.
From Rotterdam to Panama
my friends flew – true
my family enjoyed
our fortnight out in tents.
True, we were glad
to cook on an open fire.
True, we never seemed to tire
of the ghost moon
and bright stars
like ancient runes
whose patterns we read.
We'd come home dirty,
begging for a decent bed –

While our friends, hotel pampered,
smelt of lotion,
and their talk made us dream
of oceans, sands and palm trees;
we'd taste the scented breeze
of our foreign dream.
Strange then how friends
seemed to prefer to join us
for two weeks, stuck beneath canvas,
of rough wind, rain and sun.

Two weeks to feel.
To rediscover something real.

Pie Corbett

Best Friend

When my best friend died
Nothing anyone said
Helped much
And I cried and cried
And cried and cried

I'll tell you something.
We did everything together.
Both caught colds
Caught measles, caught frogs.
Got caught scrumping.

We were football crazy.
I was Beckham, he was Shearer
I'd cross the ball
He'd score the goal.
Now he's been substituted.

My best friend
Was the best holiday anyone ever had
Where the sky was an unbelievable blue.
The holiday you never wanted to end.
And then it did.

Roger Stevens

And Childhood
Was Mine . . .

Long, Long Ago

Long, long ago
When winters were real
And snow was deep,
And woollen hats
And wellies
Were worn by lads,
My mum and dad
Used to take me
For walks –
Snow walks
Cold walks
Frost-on-the-breath-walks,
With me, in between
Holding their hands
And swinging with delight
And squealing with delight
So long, long ago
When winters were real
And snow was deep
And childhood was mine.

Clive Webster

Aunt Sue's Stories

Aunt Sue has a head full of stories
Aunt Sue has a whole heart full of stories.
Summer nights on the front porch
Aunt Sue cuddles a brown-faced child to her bosom
And tells him stories.

Black slaves
Working in the hot sun,
And black slaves
Walking in the dewy night,
And black slaves
Singing sorrow songs on the banks of a mighty river
Mingle themselves softly
In the flow of Old Aunt Sue's voice,
Mingle themselves softly
In the dark shadows that cross and recross
Aunt Sue's stories.

And the dark-faced child listening
Knows that Aunt Sue's stories are real stories.
He knows that Aunt Sue never got her stories
Out of any book at all,
But that they came
Right out of her own life.
The dark-faced child is quiet
On a summer night
Listening to Aunt Sue's stories.

Langston Hughes

Houses

I remember the houses –

David Bullen's
where I used to say to his mother
'I'm hungry'
and get a sugar butty;

Norman Watkinson's next door
with the grandfather clock
watching from the stairs,
sawdust on the kitchen floor
and an old pump in the garden
groaning and coughing up
glittering water.

I'd two grandads' houses to go in,

one with a goose in the garden,
a harmonium with two pedals in the front room,
and an aeroplane propeller
propped up behind the big four-poster bed;

the other had freshly painted carts
to look at and not touch in the paint-shop,
with shafts held up high
and glistening blue and gold lettering,
next to coffins standing waiting.

The houses I visit now
are warmer and posher and neater
and less interesting.

Robert Hull

At Cider Mill Farm

I remember my uncle's farm
Still in midsummer
Heat hazing the air above the red rooftops
Some cattle sheds, a couple of stables
Clustered round a small yard
Lying under the hills that stretched their long back
Through three counties.

I rolled with his dogs
Among the straw bales
Stacked high in the barn he built himself
During a storm one autumn evening
Tunnelled for treasure or jumped with a scream
From a pirate ship's mast into the straw
Burrowed for gold and found he'd buried
Three battered Ford cars deep in the hay.

He drove an old tractor that sweated oil
In long black streaks down rusty orange
It chugged and whirred, coughed into life
Each day as he clattered across the cattle grids
I remember one night my cousin and I
Dragging back cows from over the common
We prodded the giant steaming flanks
Pushed them homeward through the rain
And then drank tea from huge tin mugs
Feeling like farmers.

He's gone now, he sold it
But I have been back for one last look
To the twist in the lane that borders the stream
Where Mary, Ruth and I once waded
Water sloshing over our wellies
And I showed my own children my uncle's farm
The barn still leaning over the straw
With for all I know, three battered Ford cars
Still buried beneath it.

David Harmer

Salford Road

Salford Road, Salford Road,
Is the place where I was born,
With a green front gate, a red brick wall
And hydrangeas round a lawn.

Salford Road, Salford Road,
Is the road where we would play
Where the sky lay over the rooftops
Like a friend who'd come to stay.

The Gardeners lived at fifty-five,
The Lunds with the willow tree,
Mr Pool with the flag and the garden pond
And the Harndens at fifty-three.

There was riding bikes and laughing
Till we couldn't laugh any more,
And bilberries picked on the hillside
And picnics on the shore.

I lay in bed when I was four
As the sunlight turned to grey
And heard the train through my pillow
And the seagulls far away.

And I rose to look out of my window
For I knew that someone was there
And a man stood as sad as nevermore
And didn't see me there.

And when I stand in Salford Road
And think of the boy who was me
I feel that from one of the windows
Someone is looking at me.

My friends walked out one summer day,
Walked singing down the lane,
My friends walked into a wood called Time
And never came out again.

We live in a land called Gone-Today
That's made of bricks and straw
But Salford Road runs through my head
To a land called Evermore.

Gareth Owen

In a Grandmother's House –
Glasgow, 1960

A grandmother's house is so different
from your own home.
The smell is nicer – like flowers everywhere.

Unfamiliar items in the bathroom,
packets of pills and potions: Aspirins and Rennies,
small boxes of corn plasters,
an undisciplined regiment of tall talc tins.
There's cellophaned soap
and towels much softer than those at home.
It's a garden, really, this bathroom,
filled with confusing smells
– summerly smells, motherly smells, safe smells.

Her bedroom (always tidy, not like mine)
is an Arabian cave filled to the ceiling
with trinkets and treasures that
catch the autumn light.
A bracelet from Blackpool,
a lace hankie brought from Singapore
when her son was a soldier there,
a matching eggcup, plate and mug
all the way from the Lake District.
And in her wardrobe
hats, furs, belts, silks, candlewicks
and photos of her dead husband.

I'd like to take some of these things home:
we don't have ornaments like these,
six wooden elephants marching
over a curved bridge;
a sculptured watermill in a large plate –
you can trace the water's path with your finger.
A brown photo of my grandfather with his
   family
(is that my great-aunt? Did this man die
in the first war or the second? Is this his medal?)
I'd like to take some of these things home:
to own your history, and to create my own.

John Rice

The Family Book

My father unlocks the family book
where the captured Victorians sit
tight-lipped, keeping their own closed counsel.
I find them caught at christenings
as the 'greats' collect with the 'latest'
and another name is tied to the family line;
or posed (but not poised) in studios,
the fathers and sons from their Sunday slumbers,
suited and sober and seemingly shy
as if their souls could be stolen away
for the price of a print on paper.

I watch my father separate the 'great greats'
from the 'great', the proud patriarchs,
the weddings and unsmiling aunts,
the fishermen released from their nets,
the light keeper and his shiny wife.
I flick back the pages and try to find
my fingerprints in their faces.

Brian Moses

Ancestors

1.
Every Friday morning my grandfather
left his farm of canefields, chickens, cows,
and rattled in his trap down to the harbour town
to sell his meat. He was a butcher.
Six-foot-three and very neat: high collar,
winged, a grey cravat, a waistcoat, watch-
chain just above the belt, thin narrow-
bottom trousers, and the shoes his wife
would polish every night. He drove the trap
himself: slap of the leather reins
along the horse's back and he'd be off
with a top-hearted homburg on his head:
black English country gentleman.

Now he is dead. The meat shop burned,
his property divided. A doctor bought
the horse. His mad alsatians killed it.
The wooden trap was chipped and chopped
by friends and neighbours and used to stop-
gap fences and for firewood. One yellow
wheel was rolled across the former cowpen gate.
Only his hat is left. I 'borrowed' it.

I used to try it on and hear the night wind
man go battering through the canes, cocks waking up
and thinking
it was dawn throughout the clinking country night.
Great caterpillar tractors clatter down
the broken highway now; a diesel engine grunts
where pigs once hunted garbage.
A thin asthmatic cow shares the untrashed garage.

2.

All that I can remember of his wife,
my father's mother, is that she sang us songs
('Great Tom is Cast' was one), that frightened
    me.
And she would go chug chugging with a jar
of milk until its white pap turned to yellow
butter. And in the basket underneath the stairs
she kept the polish for grandfather's shoes.

All that I have of her is voices:
laughing me out of fear because a crappaud
jumped and splashed in the dark where I was
    huddled
in the galvanized tin bath; telling us stories
round her fat white lamp. It was her Queen
Victoria lamp, she said; although the stamp
read Ever Ready. And in the night, I listened to
    her singing
in a Vicks and Vapour Rub-like voice what you
    would call the blues.

Edward Braithwaite

The Picnic in Jammu

Uncle Ayub swung me round and round
till the horizon became a rail
banked high upon the Himalayas.
The trees signalled me past. I whistled,
shut my eyes through tunnels of the air.
The family laughed, watching me puff
out my muscles, healthily aggressive.

This was late summer, before the snows
come to Kashmir, this was picnic time.

Then, uncoupling me from the sky, he
plunged me into the river, himself
a bough with me dangling at its end.
I went purple as a plum. He reared
back and lowered the branch of his arm
to Grandma who swallowed me with a kiss.
Laughter peeled away my goose pimples.

This was late summer, before the snows
come to Kashmir, this was picnic time.

After we'd eaten, he aimed grapes at
my mouth. I flung at him the shells of
pomegranates and ran off. He tracked
me down the riverbank. We battled,
melon-rind and apple-core our arms.
'You two!' Grandma cried. 'Stop fighting, you'll
tire yourselves to death!' We didn't listen.

This was late summer, before the snows
come to Kashmir and end children's games.

Zulfikar Ghose

And Even Now

When I was a child,
Lying in bed on a summer evening,
The wind was a tall sweet woman
Standing beside my window.
She came whenever my mind was quiet.

But on other nights
I was tossed about in fear and agony
Because of goblins poking at the blind,
And fearful faces underneath my bed.
We played a horrible game of hide-and-seek
With Sleep the far-off, treacherous goal.

And even now, stumbling about in the dark,
I wonder, Who was it that touched me? –
What thing laughed?

                                    Dorothy Livesay

The Wolf Next Door
But One

I never liked wolves,
Especially ones that lived next door but one,
Wild and fierce and very, very loud.

I liked them even less
When the wolf next door but one
Sunk its fangs into my arm and I had to go to
    hospital.

'Why didn't you bite it back?'
asked a matron who looked like
she'd have no trouble crunching the heads off
    crocodiles.

I didn't like the idea of biting wolves
Especially one that went on to bite
My sister, the bloke across the road,
The next-door neighbour . . . twice
And unsuccessfully tried to savage
my dad's toecapped wellies.

I didn't like wolves at all
Very specially ones that lived next door but one
And answered to the name of 'Cobber'.

'Cobber' – Australian slang for mate or friend.
'Cobber' – a wolf in Alsatian's clothing.

I'm just glad he wasn't called 'Satan'.

Paul Cookson

My First Dog

Prince was my dog,
no one else's.
I couldn't remember a time
when he wasn't there.

We grew up together,
roamed together,
got into trouble together,
winked at each other
and took our tellings-off
together.

He was my black-and-tan shadow,
sleeking along at my heels
tongue out,
chasing down the green hill
and the alleyway
to the corner shop.

He was my talisman;
with him I was safe.
He was my freedom,
his soft coat the cushion
of my dreams as I lay
tracing cloud
              patterns
                  in
                      the
                      sky.

And when he gashed his leg
on a rusted railing,
when my mother quietly told me
he had been put down,
he was the first black hole
in my young life.

The loneliness
of empty arms
and no warm neck
to put them around.

Patricia Leighton

Summer's End

I remember the long days,
long, hot evermore days
and the gathering of children
after school, gangland games,
and the trains under planked bridges
that sighed smoke,
as we peered through cracks.

The summer of gold days,
edge-of-the-world heat-high days;
railings that fenced our square
and one straggling rose,
that grew red in the dead of the dust,

and the rabbit, pushing his nose
through the cage on top of the shed,
long Sunday mornings with the papers read –
in the kitchen – windows steaming,
myself dreaming, kneeling to look out
at summer staying the same,
and boys who were passing calling my name.

The end of the summer,
evacuee time, with the long line of us
weaving down to the train, and parents who came
and cried, and summer's end
was a world that died.

Doris Corti

At the End of the Second World War

To celebrate the end of the War
all the lads and lasses
have gathered at the thistly meadow
for a twenty-five-a-side football match.

The unmarked pitch slopes down
to a duckweed-covered pond
where muddied cattle drink.
White goats crop the hawthorn.

Goalposts are heaped jackets,
waistcoats and flat caps.
The ball's a pig's bladder,
inflated, and tied with twine.

Endless, the game thunders on,
on into the gloaming.
It is nineteen-all
as the purple dusk deepens.

There are only two spectators
in the bomber-free sky:
an invalid-faced full moon
and a single astonished star.

Wes Magee

My Ship

When I was a lad my bed was the ship
that voyaged me far through the star-dusted night
to lands forever beyond the world's lip
dark burning olive lands of delight
across blood-red oceans under the stars
lorded by the scarlet splendour of Mars.

It is only a bed now spread with eiderdown
and the sheets merciless chains holding me down.

Christy Brown

How Do You Say Goodbye?

How do you say goodbye to a house
when you're moving forever on Saturday,
When you've lived there always – seven years,
And no matter what, they won't let you stay?

How do you say goodbye to a room
With its just-right walls and corners and nooks,
With its Snoopy curtains, all faded and blue,
And shelves for your toys, and fishtank, and books?

How do you say goodbye to the tree
That grew up so tall by your bedroom window,
That dances its leaves on your yellow walls
And lulls you to sleep whenever the wind blows?

How do you say goodbye to a street
Where you know all the hedges and places to hide,
The back-alley fence where you broke your arm,
And the hill at the end where you used to slide?

I wish I could move this house and this tree –
This year – this street – these swings;
My friends can all come and visit me,
But how do you say goodbye to things?

Lois Simmie

Trust Your Dreams

Dreamtime

A sleep-glazed sun slips through the streets
and rolls down hills and streams;
but before it leaves at close of day
it seems to pause at earth's edge to say,
Cry goodbye to your daytime world;
sing hello to your dreams.

Soon darkness cloaks the streets and parks
and only a half-moon gleams.
It hovers there like the ghost of a kite
which seems to sigh through the star-filled night,
Cry goodbye to your daytime world;
sing hello to your dreams.

Judith Nicholls

Pegasus

Tonight I woke from dreaming
And saw a shadow pass –
A horse swooped by my window
And now it pounds the grass.

His mane is pale as moonlight,
His silver feathers shine,
His tail streams like a comet,
And his starry eyes meet mine.

His mighty wings are beating,
So now I must decide
To hide my face in terror,
Or to trust my dreams . . .

and RIDE!

Clare Bevan

A Small Dragon

I've found a small dragon in the woodshed.
Think it must have come from deep inside a forest
because it's damp and green and leaves
are still reflecting in its eyes.

I fed it on many things, tried grass,
the roots of stars, hazelnut and dandelion,
but it stared up at me as if to say, I need
foods you can't provide.

It made a nest among the coal,
not unlike a bird's but larger,
it is out of place here
and is quite silent.

If you believed in it I would come
hurrying to your house to let you share my
 wonder,
but I want instead to see
if you yourself will pass this way.

Brian Patten

They Don't Know Everything

My mum and step-dad
Know everything
Or so they think
But

Only I know
The routes of alien spaceships
Criss-crossing the night sky

Only I know
The hidden art of invisibility
And how to fly

Only I know
The password to the hidden door
Behind the rakes in the garden shed

Only I know the secret tongue of lizards
And why the dragons
Are all dead

I'll never tell my parents what I've found
And when I'm grown up I'll keep these secrets
Safe and sound

Roger Stevens

Romance

When I was but thirteen or so
I went into a golden land,
Chimborazo, Cotopaxi
Took me by the hand.

My father died, my brother too.
They passed like fleeting dreams.
I stood where Popocatapetl
In the sunlight gleams.

I dimly heard the Master's voice
And boys far-off at play,
Chimborazo, Cotopaxi
Had stolen me away

I walked in a great golden dream
To and fro from school –
Shining Popocatapetl
The dusty streets did rule.

I walked home with a gold dark boy
And never a word I'd say,
Chimborazo, Cotopaxi
Had taken my speech away:

I gazed entranced upon his face
Fairer than any flower –
O shining Popocatapetl
It was thy magic hour.

The houses, people, traffic seemed
Thin fading dreams by day,
Chimborazo, Cotopaxi
They had stolen my soul away!

Walter James Turner

Dream of a Bird

You ask me, what did I dream?
I dreamt I became a bird.
You ask me, why did I want to become a bird?
I really wanted to have wings.
You ask me, why did I want wings?
These wings would help me fly back to my
    country.
You ask me, why did I want to go back there?
Because I wanted to find something I missed.
You ask me, what do I miss?
I miss the place where I lived as a child.
You ask me, what was that place like?
That place was happy, my family was close
    together.

You ask me, what I remember best?
I still remember, my father reading the
    newspaper.
You ask me, why I think of him?
I miss him and I am sad.
You ask me, why I am sad?
I'm sad because all my friends have fathers.
You ask me, why does this matter?
Because my father is far away.
I want to fly to him like a bird.

Bach Nga Thi Tran

A Feather from an Angel

Anton's box of treasures held
a silver key and a glassy stone,
a figurine made of polished bone
and a feather from an angel.

The figurine was from Borneo,
the stone from France or Italy,
the silver key was a mystery
but the feather came from an angel.

We might have believed him if he'd said
the feather fell from a bleached white crow
but he always replied, 'It's an angel's, I know,
a feather from an angel.'

We might have believed him if he'd said,
'An albatross let the feather fall,'
But he had no doubt, no doubt at all,
his feather came from an angel.

'I thought I'd dreamt him one night,' he'd say.
'But in the morning I knew he'd been there;
He left a feather on my bedside chair,
a feather from an angel.'

And it seems that all my life I've looked
for the sort of belief that nothing could shift,
something simple, yet precious as Anton's gift,
a feather from an angel.

Brian Moses

Poem for Kids

An old, old man lived down our street
as old as a tortoise with leathery feet

as old as a carp or a minstrel's harp
his eyes were dim but his wits were sharp:

he sat and watched the years go by
(perhaps he just *forgot* to die):

he sat and watched the suns go down
no one remembered when his hair was brown

(perhaps it was already white
when Waterloo men went to fight;

perhaps it was as white as frost
when Flodden field was won and lost).

I used to think he was as old
as the first drinking cups of gold

but his memories lay where they were stored
and he loved the world and he never got bored

And every night when he sank to rest
his dreams were rich, his dreams were blest.

I sometimes wondered why he seemed
so glad with whatever it was he dreamed,

and I asked him once, what his dreams were made of?
he answered, *Nothing to be afraid of:*

just memories of long-gone days
when the world moved in different ways,

just memories of things long gone:
they have passed, but I live on,

and so in the dreams inside my head
they will have a home till I am dead.

And I asked him once if he'd rather be
back when the world moved differently:

I asked him once, but all he would say
was, *Some things go and some things stay,*
and the world is a new world every day.

*

This old man had worked on a ship
and watched the billows swing and skip

in days when ships held out their sails
to catch the breezes, to dare the gales,

when the engine room was the windy sky
and the ship drove on with her mast held high

or the ship stood still and the sails hung idle
and skipper and mate were suicidal

till the first sail swelled and the first rope stirred
and the ship came alive like a waking bird;

and there was no coal and there was no oil
just the wind and compass and seamen's toil

and there was no stain and there was no scum
in the harbours where the cargoes come

no dead birds with useless wings
washed up by the tide like forgotten things

only the shove of the salt-sea air
and the cold white horses galloping there.

And I often wondered if he longed to be
afloat again on that sparkling sea

back in those clean and salty days
before the slicks and the greasy haze:

I asked him once, but all he would say
was, *Some things go and some things stay,
and the world is a new world every day.*

*

Then one day, just before he died,
he took my arm, drew me aside:

yes, just before his spirit passed
he must have thought he'd talk at last.

When I was born I don't remember
but from January to December

in every year that has gone round
since the first man walked on the ground

things were that should never have been
and sights you'd rather not have seen.

No words can ever tell man's story
without some shame, without some glory:

if you go back a thousand years
the picture neither clouds nor clears.

Our kindly earth was not so spoiled,
yet some men lazed, and some men toiled:

some men laughed and some men groaned
and one looked on while another was stoned:

yet there was goodness, too, and boldness,
to set against the greed and coldness.

It's one long tale, without a sequel
and its bad and its good are just about equal:

so what I have to say, young man,
is, Laugh and sing as much as you can:

for some things go, and some things stay,
and the world is a new world every day!

John Wain

Dreaming the Unicorn

I dreamed I saw the Unicorn
last night.
It rippled through the forest,
pearly white,
breathing a moonlit silence.

Its single horn
stood shining like a lance.
I saw it toss its head
and snort and prance
and paw the midnight air.
Its mane was like a mass
of silver hair.

My mind was wild, unclear.
I could not think or speak.
Above my head, I heard the branches creak
and then, from where I stood,
I watched it flicker off into the wood,
into the velvet space between the trees.

A sudden rush of rapid midnight breeze,
that felt both chill and deep,
awoke me from my sleep,
and there upon the pillow by my head
I found a strand of shining silver thread.

I kept that strand of mane
I keep it, still,
inside a box upon my window sill.
And when the world hangs heavy
on my brain,
it helps me dream the Unicorn again.

Tony Mitton

To You

To sit and dream, to sit and read,
To sit and learn about the world
Outside our world of here and now—
  Our problem world—
To dream of vast horizons of the soul
Through dreams made whole,
Unfettered, free – help me!
All you who are dreamers too,
  Help me to make
  Our world anew.
I reach out my dreams to you.

Langston Hughes

Index of First Lines

A grandmother's house is so different 130

An old, old man lived down our street 164

Anton's box of treasures held 162

A sleep-glazed sun slips through the streets 152

At Cheerio Point me and Sandy 69

Aunt Sue has a head full of stories 121

By St Thomas Water 47

Climbing up into my father's 92

Crossing alone 44

Do we know 6

Down our no-through road the game 77

Every Friday morning my grandfather 134

Fortune 34

Grandpa had an 61

Harvey doesn't laugh about how I stay short
while everybody grows 106

Houses I have made and loved 87

How do you say goodbye to a house 149

I could potter for hours on a lonely beach 54

I dreamed I saw the Unicorn 170

I found a well once 28

I had almost forgotten the singing in the streets   65

I kind of exploded inside   79

I remember, I remember   2

I remember my uncle's farm   125

I remember the houses   123

I remember the long days   144

If once you have slept on an island   10

I'm searching for a place   24

In a cool green rush   7

I never liked wolves   140

In the park they'd hang about   108

is   55

It was late afternoon on Christmas Day   63

It was my special place   8

It was only a box   20

I've found a small dragon in the woodshed   154

I wonder what it's like to be   110

Johnny's gone up Cefn Coed   112

Long, long ago   120

Michael and I were fishing companions   82

My best surprise   88

My father unlocks the family book   133

My mum and step-dad   156

On August evenings by the lamp-post   75

On autumn evenings the children still play in
  the park 97

Once a year 80

On the last afternoon of the holidays 84

On the stillest of still days 36

Our mother let us deal with it ourselves 68

Prince was my dog 142

Putting on my old jumper 74

Salford Road, Salford Road 127

Sometimes we'd watch it chug away 42

Such a sight I saw 70

That day when I was on the shore 12

That night 22

That's her 107

The good thing about friends 100

The stream. Our special place 30

The summer I was nine 41

This is our summer place 67

This is the way that I have to go 32

This is where I was when searching voices
  were calling me 95

To celebrate the end of the War 146

To let 57

Tonight I woke from dreaming 153

Uncle Ayub swung me round and round   137
Walking the dunes   14
was the first time   51
We climbed the hill   15
We form a secret club   102
We looked out of our bedroom at moonlight   18
We never went   114
When I was a boy   98
When I was a child   139
When I was a lad my bed was the ship   148
When I was but thirteen or so   158
When my best friend died   116
When we lived in a city   21
While she counts to a hundred   93
You ask me, what did I dream?   160

Index of Poets

Adamson, Robert 69

Bevan, Clare 153

Braithwaite, Edward 134

Brown, Christy 148

Calder, Dave 95

Carter, James 22

Causley, Charles 47

Coldwell, John 74

Cookson, Paul 140

Corbett, Pie 80, 114

Corti, Doris 144

Cowling, Sue 68

Curry, Jennifer 8

Doherty, Berlie 67, 88

Dymoke, Sue 93

Ferlinghetti, Lawrence 34

Field, Rachel 10

Finney, Eric 14, 18, 54

Fisher, Aileen 21

Ghose, Zulfikar 137

Green, Mary 42

Greygoose, David 6

Harmer, David 108, 125

Hood, Thomas 2

Hughes, Langston 121

Hull, Robert 123

Johnson, Mike 61, 110

Jones, Brian 100

Joseph, Jenny 70

Kitching, Daphne 24

Lamb, Helen 7

Lee, Brian 12, 32, 44

Leighton, Patricia 15, 142

Livesay, Dorothy 139

Magee, Wes 63, 146

Mellor, Robin 112

Mitton, Tony 98, 170

Mole, John 77, 92

Moses, Brian 82, 133, 162

Newbery, Linda 30

Nicholls, Judith 152

Owen, Gareth 57, 75, 127

Patten, Brian 154

Reeves, James 65

Rice, John 130

Simmie, Lois 149

Simpson, Matt 55

Steven, Kenneth C. 29

Stevens, Roger 116, 156

Summerfield, Geoffrey 36

Sutton, David 97

Swinger, Marian 107

Taylor, Andrew 79

Topping, Angela 87

Tran, Bach Nga Thi 160

Turner, Steve 102

Turner, Walter James 158

Viorst, Judith 106

Waddell, Philip 20

Wain, John 164

Warry, Cathy 41

Webster, Clive 120

Whitehead, David 84

Wong-Chu, Jim 51

Acknowledgements

The publishers wish to thank the following for permission to use copyright material:

Clare Bevan, 'Pegasus', first published in *Moondust and Mystery*, 2002, Oxford University Press, by permission of the author; **Christy Brown**, 'My Ship' from *Come Softly to My Wake* by Christy Brown, published by Secker & Warburg. Used by permission of The Random House Group Limited and Mary Brown; **Dave Calder**, 'Well Hidden', by permission of the author; **James Carter**, 'The Shooting Stars', first published in *Cars, Stars, Electric Guitars* by James Carter, 2002, Walker Books, reproduced by permission of Walker Books Ltd; **Charles Causley**, 'By St Thomas Water' from *Collected Poems for Children*, 1996, Macmillan Children's Books, by permission of David Higham Associates Ltd; **John Coldwell**, 'My Old Jumper', by permission of the author; **Paul Cookson**, 'The Wolf Next Door But One', by permission of the author; **Pie Corbett**, 'Holidays' and 'Conker Crazy', first published in *Rice, Pie and Moses*, 1995, Macmillan Children's Books, by permission of the author; **Doris Corti**, 'Summer's End', first published in *The Unsaid Goodnight*, 1989, Stride Publications, by permission of the author; **Sue Cowling**, 'Requiem for a Robin', first published in *What is a Kumquat?*, 1991, Faber & Faber, by permission of the author; **Jennifer Curry**, 'The Special Place', by permission of the author; **Berlie Doherty**, 'The Magical Bicycle' and 'Snow Spell' from *Walking on Air* by Berlie Doherty, 1999, Hodder Children's Books, by permission of the author; **Sue Dymoke**, 'Hiding Places', by permission of the author; **Eric Finney**, 'Boy on the Beach', first published in *Our Side of the Playground*, 1991, Oxford University Press, 'Doing Nothing Much', first published in *Another Fourth Poetry Book*, 1989, Oxford University Press, and 'In the Moonlight', all by permission of the author; **Mary Green**, 'Being Late', by permission of the author; **David Greygoose**, 'Do We Know?', by permission of the author; **David Harmer**, 'Not Just You, Me as Well' and 'At Cider Mill Farm', by permission of the author; **Robert Hull**, 'Houses', by permission of The Peters Fraser and Dunlop Group Limited on behalf of the author; **Jenny Joseph**, 'The Magic of the Brain', first published in *Bonkers for Conkers*, 2003, Macmillan Children's Books, by permission of the author; **Daphne Kitching**, 'A Place Without Footprints', by permission of the author; **Helen Lamb**, 'Going Down', by permission of the author; **Patricia Leighton**, 'My First Dog', first published in *The Works 2*, 2002, Macmillan Children's Books, by permission of the author; **Mike Johnson**, 'Gwyneth's Book of Records', first published in *Poetree* by Mike Johnson, 1985, Worcester Books, and 'Once Upon a Time and Space', both by permission of the author; **Brian Jones**, 'About Friends' from *The Spitfire on the Northern Line* by Brian Jones, published by Chatto & Windus. Used by permission of The Random House Group Limited; **Brian Lee**, 'The Shining', 'The Tunnel' and 'Going', by permission of the author; **Wes Magee**, 'The Christmas Shed' and 'At the End of the Second World War', by permission of the author; **Robin Mellor**, 'Cefn Coed' by permission of the author; **Tony Mitton**, 'Dreaming the Unicorn', first published in *Plum* by Tony

Mitton, 1998, Scholastic Press, and 'The Blue Marble', by permission of David Higham Associates; **John Mole**, 'Paradise' and 'A Better Game', first published in *The Conjuror's Rabbit* by John Mole, 1992, Blackie, by permission of the author; **Brian Moses**, 'Fishing Summer', 'Family Book' and 'A Feather From an Angel', by permission of the author; **Linda Newbery**, 'Mapping Our World' copyright © Linda Newbery 2003, by permission of the Maggie Noach Literary Agency on behalf of the author; **Judith Nicholls**, 'Dreamtime', by permission of the author; **Gareth Owen**, 'Den to Let', 'Street Cricket' and 'Salford Road' from *Collected Poems for Children*, 2000, Macmillan Children's Books, by permission of the author; **Brian Patten**, 'A Small Dragon', first published in *Love Poems*, 1992, Flamingo Books, by permission of the author; **John Rice**, 'In a Grandmother's House', by permission of the author; **Matt Simpson**, 'Dad's Shed', first published in *Somewhere in the Sky*, Nelson, by permission of the author; **Kenneth C. Steven**, 'The Well', by permission of the author; **Roger Stevens**, 'They Don't Know Everything' from *I Did Not Eat the Goldfish* by Roger Stevens, 2002, Macmillan Children's Books and 'Best Friend', both by permission of the author; **Marian Swinger**, 'Best Friends', by permission of the author; **Angela Topping**, 'Little Houses', by permission of the author; **Steve Turner**, 'Cranky, Scotty, Mooey and Me' from *Dad, You're Not Funny* by Steve Turner, 1999, Lion Publishing, by permission of the author; **Philip Waddell**, 'Home', by permission of the author; **Clive Webster**, 'Long, Long Ago', by permission of the author; **David Whitehead**, 'The Ascent of Everest', by permission of the author.